SYNCFLUENCE

HOW TO INFLUENCE YOUR TARGET AUDIENCE WITHOUT BURNING CASH

Foreword by Vijay Kasireddy
Lastword by Christian Fictoor

SYNCFLUENCE
HOW TO INFLUENCE YOUR TARGET AUDIENCE WITHOUT BURNING CASH

Foreword by Vijay Kasireddy
Lastword by Christian Fictoor

A great read for entrepreneurial marketers
- Scott Brinker, Editor, Chiefmartec.com

YAAGNESHWARAN GANESH

Notion Press

Old No. 38, New No. 6
McNichols Road, Chetpet
Chennai - 600 031

First Published by Notion Press 2017
Copyright © Yaagneshwaran Ganesh 2017
All Rights Reserved.

ISBN 978-1-947586-86-4

This book has been published with all reasonable efforts taken to make the material error-free after the consent of the author. No part of this book shall be used, reproduced in any manner whatsoever without written permission from the author, except in the case of brief quotations embodied in critical articles and reviews.

The Author of this book is solely responsible and liable for its content including but not limited to the views, representations, descriptions, statements, information, opinions and references ["Content"]. The Content of this book shall not constitute or be construed or deemed to reflect the opinion or expression of the Publisher or Editor. Neither the Publisher nor Editor endorse or approve the Content of this book or guarantee the reliability, accuracy or completeness of the Content published herein and do not make any representations or warranties of any kind, express or implied, including but not limited to the implied warranties of merchantability, fitness for a particular purpose. The Publisher and Editor shall not be liable whatsoever for any errors, omissions, whether such errors or omissions result from negligence, accident, or any other cause or claims for loss or damages of any kind, including without limitation, indirect or consequential loss or damage arising out of use, inability to use, or about the reliability, accuracy or sufficiency of the information contained in this book.

Contents

Praise for Syncfluence — vii
Foreword — ix

Introduction — 1
PART I Identifying your Influencers — 7
  1. Thought Process of a Syncfluencer — 9
  2. How Does One Get Influenced? — 14
  3. Build Your Community — 25
  4. Know Your Customer's Journey — 30
  5. Ensure Brand – Influencer Fit — 33
PART II Communication for Syncfluence — 37
  6. When Not to Make Noise! — 39
  7. It Isn't about Buying "Reach" — 43
  8. Never Get Too Flashy, Keep It Subtle — 48
  9. Simple Always Wins! — 52
10. Cultivate Cult — 55
11. The Hashtag Logic — 58
12. Sell a Conviction — 63

Contents

PART III Influencing with Product Design and Packaging   **67**

13. Design Customer Interest   69

14. Make Your UX Work for You   73

15. Get Them Hooked   76

16. The Devil Is in the Detail   79

17. Try Adding a Premium Package   85

18. Bots Are Not Always Bought!   88

PART IV Get Syncfluencing   **93**

19. Syncfluence Begins within the Organization   95

20. Go beyond Vanity Metrics   99

Lastword   *104*

Acknowledgements   *111*

Author Bio   *113*

Praise for Syncfluence

"A great read for entrepreneurial marketers. And every entrepreneur needs to be a syncfluencer. Yaagneshwaran bottles his energy and enthusiasm for the dynamics of modern marketing and influence building."

– *Scott Brinker, Editor, chiefmartec.com*

"SyncFluence is a worthwhile read for aspiring entrepreneurs intent on building a brand and influencing purchase intent."

– *Mike Quindazzi, Executive Committee, LA County Economic Development Corporation, USA*

"From moments to episodes of influence, this book connects the dots. For you! Influence your way to biz success. This book tells you how!"

– *Pravin Shekar, CEO, Krea.in, India*

Praise for Syncfluence

"In the influencer landscape, SyncFluence comes at a perfect time, showing the way forward for marketers of all stripes."

– *Avi Lambert, CEO, Photonic Public Relations, Canada*

"In SyncFluence, Yaagneshwaran simplifies the martech and influencer marketing maze by bringing down-to-earth focus on user experience (UX) and overall customer experience (CX). It is a one stop shop that goes beyond vanity metrics."

– *Prof. T.N. Swaminathan, Director of Marketing and Branding, Great Lakes Institute of Management, India*

"Yaagneshwaran's writing is practical and very insightful. Syncfluence delivers on its promise – smart ways to influence across customer touch points. A great read!"

– *Omri Shabi, Serial Entrepreneur and Director of Marketing, Woo.io, Israel*

Foreword

Growth Hacking is on everyone's agenda these days. It comes down to figuring out basic questions like: 'How to win new customers?' 'How to add more value to the existing customers?' and 'How to do this in an economical way?'

We have all seen or heard about growth hack programs that didn't work well, while some programs on the other hand that were very successful, and occasionally programs that were not only successful but seemed to expand with no effort, as if on an auto-pilot mode.

I had the chance of being part of one such program where we worked to build a small user community of about 100 people to listen in, learn and share with each other.

In a short time, the community grew 100X, product coverage increased 5X, and the program expanded across borders with regional and international chapters, and all this with little efforts from the product teams. It seemed as if the users turned out to be growth hackers, albeit unintentionally! Imagine hiring growth hackers who pay you to hack your growth.

This program happened in the year the iPhone was conceived. The social and mobile revolution was at its infancy. Today, there is an unprecedented opportunity to build, connect and engage with the users and experts, who are influencing everyone around them.

The market place for the new age communities has exploded, and is expected to grow significantly in the foreseeable future. This is where you can find all your potential growth hackers.

Imagine hiring all the growth hackers – or influencers – you can, for free, who could champion your products and services, and guide the potential users in the most profound ways. It can be as simple as it sounds, with a planned approach to influencing, or what Yaagneshwaran refers to as getting your influencers to be in sync with your belief system.

He beautifully illustrates simple but powerful principles of the art and science of influence building in the modern day. Weaving in stories and examples, Yaagneshwaran debunks many myths such as: it's not really about buying reach, but it's about reach with relevance, how marketing cannot help when one doesn't know what appeals to the customer.

Whether you are an experienced or aspiring growth hacker, there's something for everyone!

Thank you,
Vijay Kasireddy
CEO & Co-founder, Fiind Inc.

Introduction

How many times have you switched television channels during a commercial? How many times have you sensed a sales pitch coming your way and already tuned yourself out, the moment you got a LinkedIn invitation to connect with a sales professional?

Why does it happen? They seek your attention, but what they say isn't of interest to you. At times, it may not even be relevant to you.

Yet, when you switch roles and wear the hat of a marketing and sales professional, you also seek attention. You want your target audience to be influenced by your brand.

Let's say, you take the social media route. There are a lot of people hanging out on social media platforms, and some of them are your target audience, too. But still they tune out of your ads, content and communication.

Trust me, I've been there and failed several times in my attempt to seek attention. There have been times where I burnt a lot of cash trying to influence my target audience, only to see zero conversion.

When you are pressed until it hurts, you know where to look for the solution. After talking to a lot of successful peers in the startup community across the globe, and also closely following their marketing and sales operations, it was evident that the difference between the best and the rest was the ability to stay relevant, create trust and be obsessed about each and every customer. It showed in their campaigns, social media posts, events, and more.

In other words, the success of these companies was directly proportional to how much they were in sync with their customers and how personalized their influencing programs could get.

That is what Syncfluence is all about – creating synchronized influence across various touch points in your customer journey.

This book, while making no claims about being the only way to hacking influencer marketing, is an attempt to share the influence building hacks gathered based on the conversations and lessons learnt from startup founders who have been there and done that, musicians who established themselves and went on to become celebrities, successful CMOs, consultants and more.

In fact, #syncchat experiment on twitter was one such learning.

The learning is continuous and two-way, so I would love to hear your experiments, experiences, tips and tricks, and more. Feel free to email me at yaagneshwaran@fiind.com

Alright, without further ado, let us get into 'Syncfluence!'

It is not about betting on influencing channels and influencers. Maybe a good starting point is to check if you and the influencer have something in common!

A Syncfluencer first looks for common influencing interests and then checks if those are in sync with their audience.
#syncfluence

PART I

IDENTIFYING YOUR INFLUENCERS

1
Thought Process of a Syncfluencer

Imagine this scenario: You have launched a line of custom T-shirts. You sourced high-quality raw materials from the best sources, have employed the top fashionistas for the best in breed designs, and aim to be seen as a hipster brand with a premium price tag.

To get the right kind of attention for your brand, you want to leverage various mediums of communication. You conclude that having an ecommerce website is a good place to start. Now that you have the website – you need to build presence, trust and influence.

Where do you start?

How do you build an audience of people that will not only buy your T-shirts, but also become your advocates?

You might say: go social.

Or more specifically - go Instagram? Yes, it has worked for many brands and might work in this case as well.

But before deciding upon a channel, before coming up with a strategy, before beginning to find influencers for your brand – you need to answer the most important question, which is:

"Who exactly is your customer?"

Once you determine your potential buyer, you need to focus on how to be out there and get their attention.

We all have, at some point, spoken to media agencies and more often than not, they suggest, "What you need is great public relations (PR)!"

PR definitely helps, but that's not the right way to approach the problem. It is not a scalable model, either. Sadly, the cost of customer acquisition is too high and doesn't justify as an investment to your current need.

Instead of listing the channels you know and how you will leverage them – try breaking your approach into three basic questions.

1. Who exactly is your customer?
2. Where do people fitting that persona congregate?
3. What is the best option to connect with them and start conversing?

Syncfluencing is, above all else, a mindset to influence the right people at the right time with the right touch points of experience. **#syncfluence**

You might choose to do this with influencers (both genuine advocates and paid influencers), product design, pricing and how you display the price, how you bundle your offering, and more.

In simple terms, what you want to do is:

- Be genuinely desirable to your target group

- Be in front of them at the right time without being intrusive
- Engage with them and build trust

The tactical part is incidental and might change with each company, but this is how the thought process begins.

Let us begin to engineer the syncfluencing process and, if needed, re-engineer some of the existing processes.

For every action, there is an equal and opposite reaction. With social media in the scene, there is always over-reaction.
#syncfluence

2
How Does One Get Influenced?

"There are exceptional people out there who are capable of starting epidemics. All you have to do is find them."

– *Malcolm Gladwell*

There is so much discussed about influence, to the extent that some believe influence marketing is a separate domain in itself. In reality, influencing dates back to the beginning of commerce. Influencing refers to motivating the other person to do something in your favor.

In our case, the end result of our influence is to make someone spend money to buy what we sell. Not just that, we want these customers to bring more customers.

As a marketer, there are few things that are more uplifting than your product and your story coming together, with a mélange of emotion and humor.

Yet, that influence is similar to a sip of coffee going down your throat. It is brilliant and stimulating while it lasts, but isn't forever. The high of a successful event eventually melts away and you have to work your way towards the next one. Only the best in class taste success on a regular basis.

We live in a world that is continuously influencing us in one way or the other. The moment you log on to social networks, you see people posting everything from movie reviews and music album reviews to opinions on a policy announced by the government. And in most cases, our opinions are being formed without us experiencing those products or services, in other words – preconceived opinions, thanks to the influencers.

So...how was your vacation buddy?

People liked and commented a lot on our facebook stories. So I guess it was great!

So, if you want to be influential, two things have to work for you:

1. People need to associate with your story.
2. To have better control, you have to increase your influence over your target audience, so that the influence of the competitors on your target group becomes insignificant.

Let us start with the story part.

Are you the story or the storyteller?

The most important thing in storytelling is to have a clear answer to, "Are you the story or the story teller?" It seems easy at the outset, but most companies struggle, as they get caught up in between.

As Ira Glass said, "Great stories happen to those who can tell them."

Pedro Pereira, head of Big Data at SAP Middle East, during one of our conversations, said, 'As long as there are people, there will be stories, and the stories that engage are the ones that connect with people on an emotional level.'

He further added, 'It is always good to share your story with the authenticity of who you are. For example, if you are a person who is naturally humorous, it can very much be your way of storytelling. And mind you, as ironic it may sound, humor is a serious business.'

There is a lesson here. Some of us are naturally gifted in our respective professions, whether it is building software, sport, music or more. If we can communicate it in the form of a story that connects with our audience, we are on our way.

Also, storytelling needs to adapt to the platform in which it is told. During one of our sessions for an energy company, a gentleman got up to ask a brilliant question.

'We all know that storytelling has existed for ages, and is nothing new. We were doing it quite well across most traditional channels, and now suddenly the company wants to hire social media specialists and agencies. If we could be effective on traditional channels, we could handle social as well. Why do we need specialists or agencies?'

In a simplistic world, what he asked made perfect sense. However, as we navigate across mediums, we can see that each medium needs a different set of skills because each of the social platforms behaves differently from one another.

Different platforms need different skills, and different stories work on different platforms.

The platform or channel used for delivering the story is absolutely incidental to who your target audience is, where they hang out and why.

Have a purpose for influencing.

The proverb goes, "A bird in hand is worth two in the bush."

A syncfluencer says, "A business engagement is far worthier than the likes and retweets."

***

A Syncfluencer is one who influences their audience with a story to engage in business with them, and doesn't stop with engagement at events or social networking platforms.

*It's okay if you decide to put all your eggs in one basket, if you are watching the basket closely at all times. **#syncfluence***

Increasing your influence

Now that we have discussed storytelling, let us look at increasing influence.

Let us imagine a scenario where you, as a startup, are introducing new Customer Relationship Management (CRM) software. CRM as such is a mature market with lots of existing players; in other words, a red ocean.

Now, if you want to be influential in this market, you need to recognize and be in sync with the following factors:

a. Your prospects will already have an opinion on what to expect from a CRM software
b. You have no influence for now because the prospects don't know you yet
c. The influence of established players is way too much for your liking.

Okay, now what needs to change?

a. Your influence needs to increase
b. The Competition's influence has to come down

Who are the people involved in influencing your prospects?

a. Your social media and community team
b. Your competitor's team
c. People who genuinely loved your product during the Minimum Viable Product (MVP) testing stage

d. People who genuinely advocate the competitor's product
e. Paid influencers (who are usually domain consultants or domain experts) who will advocate your product
f. Paid influencers (who are usually domain consultants or domain experts) who advocate your competitor's product

Remember, established players always have more buying power than you. So, it is clearly not about mere numbers. Your influence circle needs to be more efficient and effective.

Both you and your competitor have access to the same set of paid influencers, but the differentiator is people who genuinely endorse you because they love your product.

You need to ensure a great relationship with these people, as they are perceived to be un-biased in the market. You also need to increase the number of people in this specific influence bucket. Ensure they feel valued, so that they bring in more people.

It is your responsibility to build a community around your product. And by doing so, you can even make an unhappy customer give you inputs to enhance your product rather than them writing blogs on how your product sucks.

Let us look at community building in the next chapter.

Be a Syncfluencer!!

Sometimes, all it takes is keeping your ears to the ground and knowing who loves you!
#syncfluence

Build your community and engage with them.

Have influencing components at every touch point – more importantly, the right touch points!

3
Build Your Community

"Communication leads to community, that is, to understanding, intimacy and mutual valuing."

– *Rollo May*

Community is at the core of your business. Whatever you build, you build it for people who would likely engage with you and end up becoming your customer.

To achieve a sizeable customer base, you need to establish a significant presence, both at the enterprise level as well as at the individual level. Else you are invisible.

They say, "Raise your hands to be counted or lie down and be left out." But you don't want to be raising your hands when nobody is looking. You want people to raise their hands along with you and create a wave.

Build your community. Take care of them. Love them.

They will support you, share your views and even fight for your viewpoint with the opposition. In short, they will market you for free.

A community cannot be built in a day or at the press of a few buttons. You need to sow, grow and nurture it.

Community is all about sharing common attitudes, interests and goals.

Remember that communication is a two-way street. On one hand, it is engaging people by sharing information, and on the other hand, it is about listening to new ideas and expanding the scope of your shared vision.

People are more likely to engage and share with others if they feel that their ideas are heard and considered valuable.

Effective communication showcases what you are all about and helps establish authority in your niche.

It assures your community they are a part of a professional network of talent that treats all people with the respect and maturity they deserve.

When you think of building your community, tons of ideas and suggestions will come your way from varied sources. You will get ideas ranging from meet-up events to WhatsApp groups and more. Some may fit your goals; others may not.

So, how do you build your community?

Here's one such example.

Roos Blufpand, a leading musician/band, based in the Netherlands, who is still in her early twenties, has the perfect understanding of how to build her community.

When I asked her if she focuses on a specific genre so that she can build an audience with a specific taste, she said, "That is something I would never do. It is easy to be stereotyped in the music industry. And more importantly, if I continue to play the same genre, I'll end up only seeing a small audience growing old with me, and I'll never be able to scale up my community."

She continuously experiments newer genres and believes in sharing emotions and stories through her songs. And more importantly, she performs for different sizes of audience at different ambiences.

For example, you'll find her performing in a small restaurant that can accommodate 20–30 customers, where the audience can connect with her on a personal level. At the same time, she also caters to a larger audience in theatrical setups.

She exactly knows that at restaurants, she caters to a certain audience segment, and a whole different segment at theaters. By catering to different audiences, she is not only in sync with them; she is also a syncfluencer.

Be where your audience is. Never assume that they know what they want and do not stop with giving them only that.
#syncfluence

Expectations are usually based on past experiences.

Feel free to experiment, and you'll be pleasantly surprised!

Know the pulse of your audience.
Ignorance isn't bliss at all.
Make sure it's not too late!

Shawn doesn't know Veronica has dumped him for Robert.
He's ordering flowers for her

4
Know Your Customer's Journey

"You've got to start with the customer's experience and work backward towards the technology – not the other way around."

– *Steve Jobs*

Being a bootstrapped start-up, you don't have a lot of cash to burn in the course of making yourself visible.

Hence, it becomes important for you and your influencing unit to communicate the right things at the right time to the right set of prospects.

For that to happen, you need to precisely understand the journey of your prospects and customers. You need know where exactly they are in the buying cycle.

Here are some examples of stages in the buying cycle:

a. The prospect is not actually looking for something that you offer, but stumbled upon your product during a random browsing

b. They were searching for some specific information pertaining to your product domain

c. They know what they want and are evaluating the options available

Now, where do you plug in your influencing team?

The answer to this question is asking further pointed questions such as: who exactly is seeking information? Why? What are the possible factors that influence them?

For instance, imagine you are a tourism service provider.

Who is seeking the information?

Are they a honeymoon couple seeking a getaway for a couple weeks? Are they are solo travelers who seek adventure?

Why?

What is the exact experience sought? What is the motivation?

What are the possible factors of influence?

This is an equally important question. This often regulates the depth of information to be shared by your influencer team.

In an interesting conversation with Srinidhi Hande, an avid travel blogger, he shared, "The most important thing to be communicated in a travel blog is experience.

For example, during my trip to Malaysia, I saw a never-before seen way of extracting tender coconut in a shop near Menara Towers in Melaka. I was blown over by what I saw and I wrote about it in my blog. It is not the kind of information you will find on a tourism company's site. But this is an experience that a traveler might want to soak into."

Having someone like Srinidhi as part of your community adds great value because of the depth of information he is able to share.

A prospect is more interested in knowing what to explore, what is unusual, what not to miss out, than being given a conventional time-table that says -

Kuala Lumpur - Full day Genting tour with 1-way cable car (cable car – subject to operational/weather conditions)

Pick up from your hotel at 8:30 am (post your breakfast)

Ask yourself –

How do I make the life of my customer/prospect easier today? How can I improve their experience today? What is that one step forward from what I offered yesterday?

Take care of the minute details; the bigger things will take care of themselves.

Don't be an influencer, be a syncfluencer!

5
Ensure Brand – Influencer Fit

"Your life is controlled by what you focus on."

– *Tony Robbins*

Always analyze, think through, and know the outcome you want to drive and the impact you want to create before zeroing in on a specific influencer for your marketing campaigns.

Never change your campaign goal to fit the clout of the influencer – always look for an influencer that fits your message, brand and audience.

There is often a tendency to feel the need to tap into the influencer's audience, but let it happen only if they are in sync with your core belief system and your product offering rather than going the other way around.

Here are a few parameters to consider while selecting your influencer.

(i) **Number of followers is just a number**

It is easy to think that the number of followers is directly proportional to the amount of influence, but it is not so.

There are two aspects to explore further – (a) Are all followers genuine and human (hopefully not bots?) (b) How many of these followers are relevant to you or represent your target segment?

(ii) **Evaluate their engagement**

Look beyond likes, retweets, and shares. Look at the kind of engagement, the kind of questions asked by the followers of the influencer, the depth of information provided, the kind of people (domain interests) engaging with the influencer, etc.

These aspects will give you a ballpark of the engagement you can expect for the content you request the influencer to engage upon.

(iii) **Is the content promoted? How frequently?**

Always keep an eye out for branded content/posts by the influencer. There are few things that will clearly tell you if someone is a professional influencer paid by the brand for posting content or a regular influencer who posts out of personal interest.

Usually, the brand stories shared by them and how they respond to followers will give you a macro perspective.

A litmus test would be to check if they share a lot of promoted posts. Stay away from those

influencers, as your content may get lost in the stream of their promoted content.

"Not to work with an influencer promoting your competitor" is a myth.

If the influencer is a domain expert or is known for his expertise in a particular domain or a product area and is seen to have unbiased healthy interactions with the audience, then you can choose to work with them by all means.

Like the Schrodinger's cat experiment where, until the box is opened, an observer doesn't know whether the cat inside is alive or dead – unless you really validate if the influencer is a fit with your brand, your campaign's chances of being successful will be 50:50.

Validate if the influencer is in sync with your brand values and expertise. Otherwise your will sink. **#syncfluence**

PART II

COMMUNICATION FOR SYNCFLUENCE

*Communicate according to your audience.
Not everyone reads from left to right.*

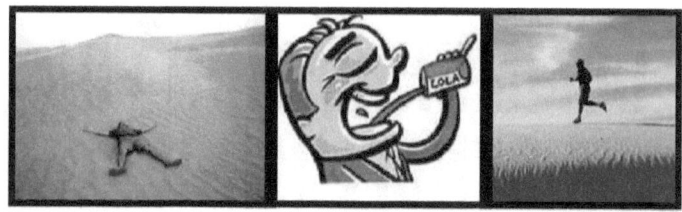

Source: Coke's failed ad in the Middle East

6
When Not to Make Noise!

"Trust is like an eraser, it gets smaller and smaller after every mistake."

– *Unknown*

Here's a story:

There was a bull that strayed into the forest in search of sweet grass. While grazing, in due course, he went deeper and deeper into the forest.

Once he was full, he got ecstatic and started bellowing. A lion passing by heard him, and pounced on him. The lion tore the bull apart and ate him up.

The lion then started roaring with pride. As pride knows no limits, the lion continued to roar louder and louder. A hunter who was passing by heard the lion, spotted him and shot him down.

Moral of the story: When you are full of bull, don't make noise.

Now, try to relate this story in the world of business. What is promotion-worthy?

Cameron Craig, the former PR expert of Apple, believed it was important to stay focused on telling your specific story despite the distractions.

The Steve Jobs-led team was always focused on telling the story of how innovative their products were and how they believed in challenging the status quo.

But on any given day, they would get bombarded with requests to write thought leadership content pieces, chime in on industry trends, invitations as guest speakers for events and more.

If the requests weren't in sync with Apple's mission, they would politely decline the opportunity. The priority was clear – be the expert, be the innovator, challenge the status quo.

Also, if you observe, their press releases and events were often reserved only for the really important moments like a new product launch or a company milestone.

While it may be frustrating for several people working on software update releases or pet projects for not getting the deserved coverage for their hard work, it earned the respect of media, prospects and customers.

The media was always confident that it was worth their time, whenever they received a call from Apple.

As a startup, you need your prospect's attention. You need your influencer's attention. For that to happen, they need to see value in not only what you offer, but also what you speak.

*Stick to your expertise. Never spread yourselves too thin. Promote only really valuable information. **#syncfluence***

Remember, there are no markets, but individuals. It's not about "messaging" but about "communicating."

Let your content be music and not noise for the recipients.

Stay in sync!

Customers and prospects see through fluff. As a startupreneur, you can't afford to be ignored.

Take a peak,
Fix the leak,
Then fill it up.

Reach out, only after knowing whom to reach out and where they are!!

7
It Isn't about Buying "Reach"

"99% of the people don't market in the year that we actually live in."

– Gary Vaynerchuk

"Yay! My hash tag is trending on twitter today," "My website has got over 10,000 hits this month" – does it sound familiar?

It surely gives you a kick and makes you look good for the day. What next?

Trending on twitter is great, but does it result in creating a following for your brand? Or does it have an effect on the sales? No.

10,000 website hits does sound cool, but does it tell you who these 10,000 people are? No.

I had the opportunity of discussing twitter trends with Sarath Babu, a lifestyle blogger and social influencer. He nailed it: "Create quality content. Content that provides valuable information to your audience, and not a sales pitch. What is the point of trending a hash tag if it doesn't lead to a desirable action? Spend more time creating something useful for the customer, and less time promoting it!"

Now, this is the mindset of a syncfluencer.

He further added, "Remember, it is not about buying "reach." What is the point of becoming suddenly visible to 10,000 people who are not even remotely connected to your industry domain?"

It is worth analyzing only when you attempt to communicate with a relevant audience. Then check what is happening on a per-prospect basis and categorize. For example, you can replace measuring the total number of pageviews on your website in a given month, with the number of pageviews per prospect and returning customer.

Have the right reasons to bring in an influencer. Influencers help you reach a specific niche and sharpen your marketing efforts.

When you decide to involve a paid influencer, the first thing to look for is the passion they share for your industry domain/sector/category. However, it doesn't necessarily mean that you shouldn't involve influencers from other domains.

For example, if you're launching a new car, it doesn't mean you invite only motor experts. You may also invite children and family members who don't drive. The can also be your influencers. Why?

Remember the customer journey – it is important to identify and cater to all the decision makers involved in the buying process.

A motor expert might test-drive your new car, and derive at the pros and cons from a performance and utility standpoint, whereas others look at the comfort levels, safety measures and so on. Buying a car is a collective decision.

It's not about buying "reach." It's about reaching the buyers. **#syncfluence**

It's not about how many followers you have. It's about opening the hood and knowing who these followers are!

Converse –
Go with the flow.
Not forced, not coerced.
Subtle. Simple. Focused.

8
Never Get Too Flashy, Keep It Subtle

"People over-estimate what they can accomplish in near term and under-estimate what they can accomplish in long term."

– *David House*

The human brain processes data coming from various senses and turns this data into information that we can act upon.

Hence, what we see around us is essentially a function of our optical system transmitting visual signals to our brain, and the brain comprehending it.

The interesting thing to note here is the optical system does not send a continuous stream of data, but in short pulses. The brain cycles through the images at a certain rate which is fast enough to let us perceive most of the movement around us. According to scientific research, the brain has a cycle rate that is equivalent of a camera running 60 frames per second.

Though it seems quite fast at the outset, it is pretty slow compared to an ordinary housefly, which can detect and react to movement in about 100 nanoseconds due to its high-speed brain.

How is this relevant to a marketer?

In a word – "Distraction."

For example – let's take the case of a frog catching a fly with its tongue vs. us, humans trying to catch a fly.

Why is the fly too fast for us despite us having a developed brain whereas a frog can manage it with ease?

It is because the frog is tuned to hunting the fly. A frog cannot visually process anything that is motionless. It will focus on snatching an insect in motion, even if there are a hundred dead bugs next to the frog.

The frog knows what it is looking for. It is not distracted even an iota.

In comparison, the human mind is easily distracted. Before a content writer finishes a page of content, there are chances they have scrolled through their Facebook and Twitter feeds several times.

Here's the important part.

You might scroll past hundreds of posts and you might ignore flashy promotions, but you take notice of the subtle things. The mind is constantly scanning things around us and across platforms almost involuntarily, yet, at the same time, notices subtle changes.

Are you able to resonate with some of these examples?

You look at your car speedometer almost always exactly after it crosses 100 km/hr.

You notice the changed user interface (UI) of Facebook without a need for an announcement.

In a catchment area of several retail outlets, you exactly notice when there's a new outlet.

Moral of the story is:

You don't need to roll out a laundry list of new product features, instead you can tell your prospect on a call –

'Hey, John, great news – thought you'd want to know – based on your feature request, we managed to convince our product team to include it as part of our next version release. So fast-forward six months of effort, we now have it. Upgrade without any additional cost today!'

It's not about what new features you came up with. It's about if you enable people in noticing it!

Don't brag. Don't announce. Put it across subtly in a casual conversation.
#syncfluence

9
Simple Always Wins!

The election of Donald Trump as the President of the United States of America in November 2016 was a result that contradicted the outcome predicted by every poll and expert.

In fact, going by the amount of time and money invested on the predictive market research, you can say that it was an epic fail.

Why was Trump able to win despite team Hilary having charted out detailed policies?

People seldom make decisions based on data. Decision-making is emotional in most cases.

Look at Trump's messages vs. Hilary's:

When asked about immigration policies, which often comprises complex nuances to be taken into consideration, he said, "I'll build a wall," meaning he would make immigration of people in the country almost impossible.

He capitalized on the fear and anxiety of American citizens about their economic future, who saw immigration of foreign talent and goods as a threat.

On the other hand, Hilary had an immigration policy with nine bullet points. It was comprehensive, of course, but didn't have any recall value.

If you ask the voters about the immigration policies, the easiest recall for the word "immigration" was "wall." Trump had further tapped on the voters' emotions by promising to "Make America great again."

***

As marketers, far too often, we tend to focus on product features, factual details, components and so on. For a customer, what matters is the experience. Keep it as simple as possible to resonate.

Yes, it is of course important to educate your customer – but what's more important is to understand that you sell confidence first, and the product later.

It is all about getting an opportunity to solve a customer's problem, and it starts with getting them to believe that you can.

Keep your communication simple and uncomplicated. Know your customer as much as your spouse. It's not easy, but it is a must.

The devil is in the detail, but let the detail be under the hood. Keep the experience smooth and simple. #syncfluence

The journey of a syncfluencer is from the heart to the brain to the wallet. Plain and simple! **#syncfluence**

10
Cultivate Cult

Rap, EDM and Heavy Metal have gained a cult status over time. What is worth noticing is that these music sensibilities are also an acquired taste.

All you need is a group of people who believe in what you believe, to make it a rage. Once it becomes a rage, it spreads and then becomes a tradition.

For example - the once notorious Norse pirates were later celebrated as Vikings, who are popular historical figures even today. Mythological reference and their appearance in pop culture gave Vikings their cult status.

So, how does one go about gaining a cult status?

It was the last Wednesday of August in 1945, in the Eastern parts of Spain, when a disgruntled group of youngsters rioted and attacked the city councilmen with tomatoes during a town celebration. People pelted each other with tomatoes until the local forces ended the battle.

If you see an opportunity – grab it with both hands!

The following year, smart vegetable merchants stocked more tomatoes in expectation, some even offered home delivery. As expected, during the town celebration, the young group again started a tomato battle, this time having brought the tomatoes from home.

This time around, more people participated in the pelting and it was called La Tomatina in Spanish.

The celebration was banned in the early 1950's. In fact, in 1957, as a sign of protest, some people conducted a cremation ceremony for a tomato.

They carried a coffin with a huge tomato in it and accompanied it with a band that played funeral marches. Banning it only made it more popular, causing more people to have frenetic feelings over the ban.

This is how the La Tomatina Festival, which has a cult status in Spain, was finally allowed to become an official festivity.

In 2002, La Tomatina of Buñol was declared as a festival of International Tourist Interest by the Spanish Department of Tourism due to its success.

Ban as a strategy?

The La Tomatina ban was one of the earliest contributions to today's inclusion of ban as part of promotions. And we have seen that it pays off, often initiating viral marketing through word of mouth. The opportunities are everywhere, you just need to spot it.

Syncfluencers never miss an opportunity. They cultivate cults. **#syncfluence**

11
The Hashtag Logic

On a daily basis, several topics trend on social media. Take a look at Twitter for example – you'll see ten topics trending at any given point of time.

Take a closer look. Is there a noticeable pattern in these trending topics?

Is it that the trending list is usually divided into five hashtags, and five key words?

Good observation, but a little more. What are the trends that make you click and explore further?

Let's say that the trending topics for the day are as follows:

#TNJallikattu

#LITClassyCombos

Raees pre booking starts

#AircelSavetheTiger

AmazonGreatIndianSale

TataHexa

Brad Pitt and Angelina

Apple watch

\#ExclusiveonShopClues

\#ThankyouObamas

It is likely that you would not click on the topics that appear blatantly promotional in nature.

Sometimes, there might be something that you find interesting, but you choose to stay away because you suspect an ulterior motive.

For example, let's take #AircelSavetheTiger - a campaign by the telecom service provider Aircel to create awareness on the decline in the number Royal Bengal Tigers in India and the need to save them from extinction.

Clearly, it's a cause you want to support, but the brand name association in the hashtag has made it a branding exercise. In other words, the authenticity of the case is lost.

Rajasekar KS, General Manager – Marketing of Bharat Matrimony, during our meeting at his office, put it precisely when he said, "You miss the whole point of influence when you try to endorse your brand. If you stand for a cause, stick to the cause. Intent is more important than content."

He added, "You need to facilitate a conversation rather than pushing a message. Today's conversation will fill tomorrow's coffers."

In fact, the marketing team at Matrimony lives and breathes the ideology. They neither use their brand name in hash tags nor sound sales-y in their conversations.

Here's a sample conversation taken from their Twitter account:

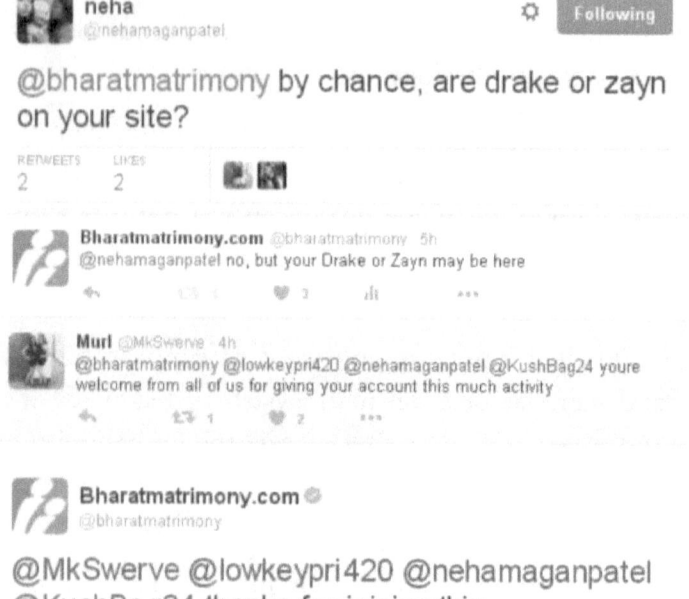

Believe in the power of serendipity. If you can surprise your prospects or customers in a pleasant manner, magical things can happen.

The human brain often finds unexpected pleasure more rewarding, than the expected ones. Let go of the conventional path. Customers know that you are in business for a reason, so avoid being pushy.

Transformation always precedes transactions. If you can offer a great experience, transaction will be a byproduct.

Customer experience (CX) is the biggest differentiator and the most impactful touch point that makes or breaks a deal.
#syncfluence

In most cases, people don't buy the product; they buy the promise.

It's not sexual intercourse that gets people excited, but the possibility of it.

12
Sell a Conviction

"Logic makes people think. Emotion makes people act."

– Zig Ziglar

What is the single most important job of a sales person? Selling their product? Making revenue?

These are important, yes, but one thing precedes all of these. Conviction. Sales people need to sell a conviction.

A belief. A story. An emotion. A feeling.

How many times have you told yourself that organic food is good for your health and paid extra bucks while you were in a super market?

Who told you sunflower oil is good for your health? The man dressed like a doctor in the TV commercial?

Is organic food really good for your health? Do we really know it? Do we really look at every ingredient on the package before we put them into our trolley? Or when you add them to your cart while shopping online?

Honestly, the answer is – we do not know. Even if you buy it directly from the farmer, there is no way to confirm if it was really organic farming.

Or for that matter, when some people go to a restaurant and order chicken, they tend to look out for HALAL certification. Do they really know how the chicken was slaughtered? No.

So, what we actually buy is a feeling. A feeling that satisfies our ego as we think we are buying products in the best interest of our family. A price we pay to buy a conviction.

Let's take the case of organic food. Kroger, the US based supermarket giant, in 2015 started to see the shift toward natural and organic in its sales data. With that insight, they went on to build Kroger's own organic brand, called Simple Truth, which led them to a double-digit growth rate in sales by the end of that year.

Look at how Hubspot defined inbound marketing. They told the whole world a story of how outbound marketing approach would be ignored and wiped out.

Regardless of whether people bought Hubspot marketing automation software or not, they bought the concept.

The point in case is – sell the story. Sell a belief system. Show the world that you are living your story. Show them how it helped you succeed.

All you need is people to believe in your brand, your product and your story. The rest will be word of mouth.

Regardless of time, word of mouth has, and will remain, the most powerful weapon in marketing.

When you are giving reasons, you are trying to convince. When you are convinced, you breed conviction.
#syncfluence

Syncfluence can happen only when everyone in the organization jumps on to the bandwagon.

Everyone needs to play their role in syncfluence building. You cannot leave it to the marketing and sales department alone.

Everyone in the organization is a designated sales enabler. It is like enlightenment — it is always there; you just have to realize it.

PART III

INFLUENCING WITH PRODUCT DESIGN AND PACKAGING

How many of you check your phone in the middle of the night (almost involuntarily) although you just woke up for a glass or water, or to visit the loo?

What influences you to do so?

13
Design Customer Interest

"Great design will not sell an inferior product, But it will enable a great product to achieve maximum potential."

– *Thomas Watson*

In most cases, it is very hard to articulate why someone likes or dislikes a product. What makes it more mysterious is that not many people can predict the behavior of future customers or a future buying behavior.

Ask yourself the following questions to get started. Check how best you can answer these questions.

- How does a new product get noticed?
- What makes your product attractive to your target market? (This is not what you think is your product's USP or internal views from your organization)

It is extremely important to find the right balance between novelty and familiarity. The right balance might vary from company to company based on who their customers are.

Are your customers attracted to novelty and innovation? Do they expect you to come up with something new all the time? Or are they overwhelmed by the non-familiarity of your product, so it leads to rejection? What does it mean to product design?

Take a look into the aspects that cater to the user's attention and emotion.

Design products to get the customers' attention. Base the product on the kind of emotional relationship you want them to build with your product.

Neuroscience reports show that certain preferences are universal, for example – most people prefer curved lines and edges, compared to straight lines and sharp edges.

Make it easy to comprehend without the need for the consumer to engage in deliberate thinking.

Enable the right emotion.

To understand the buyer's thought process, the executives at PepsiCo's Frito-Lay unit tested commercials, products and packaging in the U.S. and overseas. They had prospects wear electrode-studded caps to capture their behavior.

They discovered that matte beige bags of potato chips picturing potatoes and other "healthy" ingredients in the snack didn't trigger the anterior cingulate cortex

– an area of the brain associated with feelings of guilt, compared to the shiny bags with pictures of chips.

The experiment helped them in deciding to move away from the shiny packaging in the U.S.

Ask yourself – are you shouting at, boring or seducing your customer?

*Everybody has an addiction; attract the ones who are likely to be addicted to the value you offer. **#syncfluence***

*It is not who you are underneath,
it's what you do that defines you.*

— *Rachel Dawes (Batman)*

14
Make Your UX Work for You

"Success is the sum of small efforts, repeated day in and day out."

– Robert Collier

If there is madness, then there is a definite method to it. If you remember the words of the Joker from the movie Dark Knight, he says, "Madness, as you see, is like gravity – all you need is a little push."

Now apply that analogy to get a dipstick on every touch point of your product's user experience (UX) and overall customer experience (CX).

A great UX is like a good joke – you will never have to explain it.

Ask yourself if the UX of your product contributes and synergizes in delivering a great CX. This is where we need to tread carefully. Many a time, what you think attracts your customer the most might turn out to be exactly the opposite.

Take a look at these statistics from Kissmetrics:

i. 93% of consumers consider visual appearance and color to be more important than texture, sound or smell.

ii. 85% of consumers cite color as a primary reason for them to purchase a particular product.

iii. 42% of shoppers base their opinion of a website purely on design.

iv. 52% of shoppers do not return because they dislike the overall aesthetics of a website.

v. Color increases brand recognition by 80% because it is tied to consumer confidence.

In most cases – very few companies take these factors into account during the product ideating and designing stage.

Let us take ecommerce brands for example. We often tend to spend great amount of time, money and effort on speed, solution to a specific UX problem, ease of use, and more in an effort to create a seamless experience, but miss taking into account the customers' emotions at various touch points.

Yes, it is great to be data driven and not ignore analytics. But – you also need to remember that influence happens at an emotional level. It is that split second which drives the decision to purchase.

Brand loyalty is an emotion. It is like your native language or culture – something that gives you a sense of belonging.

Let your user experience design become an emotional experience design. Place human understanding and emotion at the core of every brief, and make sure your team understands the "why" before getting into how.

Never miss a single touch point.

*Design for the homerun, but go one base at a time. **#syncfluence***

15
Get Them Hooked

"There are only two ways to influence human behavior – you can manipulate or inspire."

– *Simon Sinek*

Most of us feel the need to check our Facebook account every now and then. Many a time, we do that even without a notification. Why does this happen?

From another perspective – How does Facebook manage to drive this behavior in you? Is there a method to this madness?

Absolutely!

Nir Eyal, in his brilliant book, "Hooked," covers extensively the science of habit forming and how behavioral designing is done. It is a must-read for every entrepreneur, especially the ones who are building product-oriented companies.

However, here's an attempt to give you a gist of what Nir has discovered, by continuing the Facebook example.

How is the Facebook frequenting habit formed?

There is a trigger that leads you to an action. For example, a colleague who is already on Facebook tells you that he was able to connect with his school friend whom he last saw during his childhood.

You, too, see the possibility of connecting with some of your long-lost friends. Your colleague sends you an email invite; you click on the link and end up joining Facebook.

Then, with time, you become friends with a lot of people, and in many cases, these are people you might have never met before.

On the other hand, there are terabytes of information shared easily all over Facebook. This is where you move from action to reward.

You find a photo shared by your Facebook friend to be interesting; hence, you click on it. Bam!! You end up reaching their Instagram profile. You are dazzled by the collection of images posted by them. There you have it – a reward for your action.

The next step is the most important one, which product companies strive for – investment from the users.

Investment need not necessarily mean monetary investment. It can be time, effort, information and more.

For example, in this phase, you start posting content, sharing content, and more importantly you start stating your preferences for the information you would like to receive, your areas of interest, and you even start inviting your friends, recommending them to try out Facebook.

***

Facebook did not get billions of users by chance. The baits were part of the design. Habit-forming technology has been in existence for a long time.

What happened throughout the stages was that you took the baits one after another and landed into the web.

With the influx of smart phones and tablets proliferating across the world, it is only getting easier by the day to access data more than ever, to custom-influence your customer based on their preference.

Applying this to your scenario:

Ask yourself –

Who is the intended user of your product? What were they doing before they start using your product?

Can you place a trigger in that space that will make them jump onto your product?

How can you enable them to share their preferences with you – so that you can offer them a better experience based on individual preferences?

Can your product be in sync with its users? Is the product influencing the right behavior?

Are you syncfluencing?

16
The Devil Is in the Detail

"It's the little details that are vital.

Little things make big things happen."

– *John Wooden*

When it comes to customer experience, the devil is in the detail. No two customers are the same. In short, one size doesn't fit all.

Yes, you need to have a scalable marketing model but you need to ensure you haven't taken customer experience for granted.

Let's take Domino's Pizza as a case example. If you have ever ordered pizza using the Domino's app, you might have observed the following:

The app allows you to build your pizza with an incredibly simple interface, by allowing you to add or replace toppings, change bases, sauce, etc.

Additionally, they also offer a multi-channel tracking of your pizza's preparation, baking, dispatch and ready to collect status.

From there, they then have an omni-channel reach out to you with integrated SMS & emails, letting you know when your pizza is ready for delivery.

Now, comes the personalization part:

The next time you order, you will slickly receive a text message offering you a discount if you ordered over a certain price amount. The point to note here is that Domino's marketing engine realizes that you are a live prospect currently engaging on their website or app.

Doesn't a timely discount offer as an SMS feel brilliant?

However, there are a few things that can go wrong, which can put you off.

Imagine you entered the discount code provided to you and you received a response saying the offer was only for collection and not for home delivery?

Another scenario - You received a promotional SMS, which triggered an interest in you to have a pizza night. You go to the store and they tell that the offer is valid only for online orders.

Why send an offer that you cannot use as a walk-in customer, despite the fact that they gain a margin by not having to offer home delivery?

The entire app experience, web experience and customer sentiment that Dominos built – all this could be blown away in a minute!

So the message is – dive into the details. Ensure what you offer is relevant to every customer you are dealing with at that point.

The judgment of customer experience is very much like how readers judge the editor of a novel. Slightest of oversights can cause harm to your brand.

Scale up sensibly. Ensure your communications are relevant to every customer.

Observe. Get insights. Use it to facilitate an outcome. Create an impact. ***#syncfluence***

When you do not know what appeals to your customer, no marketing can help you. Syncfluence is all about knowing that appealing factor, and catering to that.

Have you seen companies offering product/service subscription with multiple options for customers to choose from?

There's always an option that says "best value" or "most sought," which is priced between the highest package and the lower packages, seemingly offering the best of both worlds.

Is it just to influence you to choose that option? Does the company not want to sell the premium option? There's more to it.

17
Try Adding a Premium Package

"Sometimes life gives us lessons sent in ridiculous packaging."

– Dar Williams

There is a misconception that if you price something in the premium range, it is difficult to sell it. Although the risk is high when you premium price your offering, the returns are high, too.

We tend to overcomplicate our pricing methodology, assuming buyer's decisions are rational. In reality, it is hardly so. It is all about influencing your buyer with the right touch points.

Influence building shouldn't be an after-thought. You need to build synchronized influence – syncfluence, as a practice at every stage. Let's look at packaging in this chapter.

When you offer product packages, often the packaging and pricing are logically based on what you offer in each of the package. For example, you may have silver, gold and platinum package–silver is the stripped-down basic version, gold is the "value for money" option, and platinum is the premium one.

The preferred option by your customer in most cases would be gold, and it seems logical, as it offers the best of both worlds and appears to be value for money.

But is the decision actually logical? Does a customer's mind work exactly that way?

While talking to Naveen Valsakumar, the CEO of NotionPress, the self-publishing platform provider, he said, "For a long time, we were offering four packages on our website, namely – Silver, Gold, Diamond, Sapphire. Diamond was the best-selling package."

He added, "But we knew that our authors needed more to establish themselves in the literary world and so we encouraged more people to choose the Sapphire option. We also knew that purchase decisions weren't always logical. Buying something is often driven by emotion, whether you agree or not. With that in mind, we went for a gamble - we added another package – 'Ruby.'

The results were amazing. While the Diamond still got a lot of buyers, authors started to look at Sapphire as the one that offered best value."

What made people choose the package that earlier seemed to be the costlier option? It is because the 'Ruby' package now made "Sapphire appear to be a reasonable compromise."

Try Adding a Premium Package

On another note, you may be even surprised to see that the new premium package added might have its own audience.

And if that happens, don't be afraid to add another premium option. Always be in sync with the sentiments of your customer.

Pricing low to make your customers stay is like stopping your watch to make time stand still.

Great products with great built-in influence potential need smart packaging to be syncfluential.
#syncfluence

Some of the best minds in the world today are after Facebook likes.

*Great people think alike
…but not about a 'like!'!*

18
Bots Are Not Always Bought!

"If we don't take care of our customers, someone else will."

– Unknown

Bots are everywhere. Since offering a great customer experience is something you don't want to compromise upon, you might pose a Shakespeare styled question:

To bot or not to bot?

It is a fair question, as thanks to the advent in technology, the answer for everything is one search away for customers. All kind of information is available at the tip of their fingers on their smartphone. So, where does the bot come in the picture?

Engagement, Automation and Experience!

For example, if you log onto Amazon.com, there is a list of products that are bundled under the "Recommended for you" section. It makes your life easy as a customer, because suggestions are made based on your browsing and shopping history. Further, when you are about to buy something specific, Amazon again suggests "people who bought this, also bought this," which is usually an upsell of related products.

We know that it is automated and the suggestions are based on algorithms, yet we are okay with it. Why?

Well, because it enables our journey as a customer.

How does the bot actually influence you as a customer?

Step 1: It non-verbally tells you that Amazon knows you as a customer and understands your preferences. It presents you with things based on your interest.

Step 2: Upon getting into a product category, it tells you "I know you are smart, here are your choices, I'm sure you'll get a deal"

Step 3: In case you aren't buying, it asks you to "Add to wish list" (subtly encouraging you to come back and buy)

But there are some really bad usages of bots that you need to stay away from.

For example:

1. Never buy fake social media followers (bots quickly spike your number of followers but no engagement ever happens)
2. Never excessively automate your social media posts, show that there's a human behind those handles.

Chat bots are on the rise; use them to enhance the customer experience, not for operating at your convenience.

Most mobile and web-based bots are a mix of:

- Scripts (PHP, Ruby, JavaScript, and others)
- JSON data
- APIs and HTTPS connections to interface with the server
- The cloud (typically for storage)

And interactive bots are usually a mix of varied degrees of Artificial Intelligence (AI) and Machine learning—which help bots improve their own performance over time based on customers and data.

It is advisable to intervene the automation, every now and then, for a smooth customer experience.

Bots are bought until they're not seen explicitly as bots.

PART IV

GET SYNCFLUENCING

A syncfluencer doesn't act without thinking.
More importantly, they act.
On time, every time.
Many a time, before time.

19

Syncfluence Begins within the Organization

Being in sync with the goal of your company is a habit; it begins within the organization and flows across the organization.

It is the biggest tool to executing your strategy well. Do not let your culture eat synchronicity for breakfast.

    a. **Syncfluence begins with the outcome you want to drive.**

        Ensure your influencers and customer objectives are in sync with the outcome you are chasing to ensure a seamless syncfluential experience.

    b. **Get your internal CX efforts in sync.**

        Mapping your customer journey and developing your customer persona cannot be disjoint agendas.

        Get everyone working on your product design and CX to be in sync with your plan to influence your customer in their decision-making.

        Assign CX stakeholders to ensure this collaboration happens.

c. **Know what your customer persona is seeking.**

Do not push your message down your customer's throat. Communicate. Deliver value by helping them with solutions to their problems before they ask you.

Go beyond keyword searches.
Dive deep; be in sync.
Know what they are interested in.
Listen.
Know what they are talking about.
Syncfluence.

Be at the right place at the right time.
More importantly, capture the right information.
Use it rightly.

A drunken person often uses a lamppost for support, not for illumination.

Sometimes we tend to use statistics likewise.

Isn't its actual purpose more important?

20
Go beyond Vanity Metrics

"There are three kinds of lies: lies, damned lies, and statistics."

– Mark Twain

Be careful not to rely on vanity metrics when you are assessing your influence on your target market.

Vanity metrics are usually about numbers that give you nothing more than an ego boost. They include things such as the number of likes, shares, number of views a video gets, etc.

In other words, very rarely do they truly correlate to the things that really matter.

For example, if you are a software product company and want to build an influential community – look at the number of active users, know who they are, keep tabs on what are they engaging on and the kind of information they share.

Focus on statistics that tie to specific and repeatable tasks that are in line with the goals of your business.

That way you can work on improving the things that customers are looking for.

Tracking metrics that aren't aligned with your goals is a waste of time and can give you a false sense of security.

Identify power users – the users who drive conversations about your product and vouch for you when someone is search for a product similar to what you offer. These are the users who will have your back when the odds are against you.

Josh Kopelman, of First Round Capital, recently advised, "The real data is retention and repeat usage."

Similarly, when you are trying to identify an influencer, here are some parameters to look at:

- Look for large, engaged audiences, not traffic (engaged being the keyword).
- Make sure your influencer has similar goals and interests to your specific niche.
- Ensure that the influencer shares content often. Seek out blogs that are in existence for a long time and have regular engagement in terms of comments.

When interacting with influencers, stay away from shallow praise and non-meaningful posts. Have a clear goal, and keep it professional – influencers will appreciate it, too.

*Do not measure anything that doesn't give you an insight on what action to take next, and what outcome the action aligns to. **#syncfluence***

Set expectations,
Challenge your influencers,
Challenge your communication team,
Challenge your product development team,
Ensure they are in sync with you.
Bundle it together.
Syncfluence!!

To sum up,

You need to influence from every touch point.

The moment is now.

Let's syncfluence.

Lastword

"To Be, or Not to Be… That Is the Question."

– William Shakespeare

It is pretty safe to assume that most people across the globe are familiar with this dialogue, spoken by Prince Hamlet in Shakespeare's play, 'Hamlet.' Though this play was written in the 1600s, the words are relevant even today and more so in relation to syncfluencing.

First of all, I'm honored and privileged to write the last word for Syncfluence – the second book in the MarketingSync series, which is a sequel to "Is Your Marketing In Sync or Sinking?"

In that book, I had touched upon the 'current dynamic business ecosystem' and how you can make sure that your organization is flexible enough to steer clear from potential dangers caused by the continuous changes in the ecosystem.

Syncfluencing is getting to the next step. Probably, a little more demanding.

Being a Syncfluencer rocks!

Prepare to feel like a rockstar. You are going to be able to move crowds, build meaningful connections with potential customers, and build a solid community.

You will feel loved and be able to give love back to your audience. You might sell your merchandise by 'pushing the right (emotional) buttons.'

However, there is a method to get there. And Yaagneshwaran has covered most of it in the book.

I tell myself everyday:

> ***"Don't try or be desperate to become what/who you are not (and never will become)."***

If I have learned something from my 20 years in marketing & consulting across geographies and industries, it is this one thing that tends to separate the best from the rest –

The most successful entrepreneurs, CEOs, and Directors LIVE their brand; their story can really identify themselves with their target audience. They precisely know where they 'hang out,' be it online or offline, so they can engage with their audience in many environments, in their language. They understand and cater to their needs when they need it, and how; on time, every time.

And personally, I learnt things the hard way. Further to being on point with product-market fit and sweating it out on your marketing operations, some projects have failed. This helped me realize even more that successful companies are not built without the founder's passion in the domain in which the company operates.

The investors who bet their money on you, the customers who are willing to try out your products even when you are a newbie, do so as a result of the promise they see in you. And often this goes beyond facts and figures.

Stop and ask yourself – *is your heart in it*? Are you in sync with your journey ahead?

In fact, this introspection led me to focus on the domains close to my heart – marketing, music and events.

And it shows. My eyes sparkle and the passion is palpable when I talk to customers or peers. Hence, people connect on an emotional level. It is less about building projects and more about building relationships. Clients re-engage for more projects, and it becomes fun working with them, once the relationship is established.

Build a community you'd want to be part of yourself!

One of the key messages shared in this book is that the journey of a syncfluencer is from the heart to the brain to the wallet.

You need that 'special something' that resonates with your audience and also inspires your influencers.

So, how do we go about it? Here's a blueprint that has worked for me.

1. Pick an audience you can relate to; a group you'd want to be part of.

2. Know where those folks 'hang out' online or offline, know who/what influences them.

3. See if you have a product or service that your audience might be interested in, or simply ask them!

4. Tell your story, and make them feel a part of it.

5. Keep the dialogue going, build a community.

6. Give genuine attention to the people in your community. They are not walking bundles of cash, they are your fans, the people that tell their friends that you rock.

7. Make a visual map of all the ways people within this community are influenced and who are the 'stakeholders' involved in this (we have developed the "MarketingSync Stakeholder mapping workshop" purely for this.)

8. Approach relevant influencers and inspire them, so that they solve your problem of getting in front of your target audience.

9. Give love, energy and have fun. Keep tweaking and adjusting your products/business models based on the feedback coming from your community.

And remember: Never try to be something you are not.

Becoming a Syncfluencer is just a few steps away!

Now that you have chosen to talk to and eventually do business with a group of people you understand, you have gotten pretty close to becoming a syncfluence rockstar!

You can genuinely relate to your audience now, and they can relate to you. You speak their language, and you know what they want and need. You have the 'ammo.'

CX is everything

Make sure you have built awesome customer experience (CX) that enables your prospects and customers journeys.

Remember the rule: You have to love your customers and prospects, for them to love you back!

It sounds easier than it actually is. You have to find the perfect balance in engaging with them, know the frequency of contact your audience prefers, and build a predictive intelligence into what they might want at different moments.

Take small steps; keep your experiments agile rather than overwhelming them with loads of information that is not well thought through.

Treat them like you would treat a good friend or girlfriend: give them something to look forward to, but don't 'over-promote or brag' what you plan to do for them. Do it, show them your appreciation. Surprise them! Never underestimate the power of serendipity.

Also know that for your customer – you can be a star one day, but they can also part ways if they don't feel valued any longer.

They say – detailing is everything in retailing

Never ever disregard the details. Look beyond bills and sales.

If not, your efforts end up becoming:

- A waste of money
- A waste of resources
- A frustrating engine

Time to be a syncfluencing rock-star

You are about to rock the crowds with tunes they want to hear, tunes that will move them. The only thing you have to do is stay true to yourself, and true to your audience.

The careers of famous rockstars weren't built in a day. Spend time with loyal fans, stick to your passion and vision. Never (ever) give up. Your products or services deserve to rock your industry for a long time.

Happy exploring!

Regards,

Christian Fictoor
Co-Founder, MarketingSync & iGNITE! Music

Acknowledgements

Syncfluence is a compilation of influencer marketing experiences, gleaned from all corners of the world; great brands like PwC, SAP, marketing experts, practitioners, consultants, CEOs and CMOs, personalities that have become brands and more.

I am dedicating this book to all my gurus, thought leaders in the field of marketing and martech professionals, who are building amazing products for future marketers.

Thanks to –

Naveen Valsakumar, who initiated me into writing marketing books.

Anuja Surve and Swati Hegde, my editors, for being the linchpin in the making of this book. I cannot thank them enough for their patience and for being the final arbiter in ensuring that the book is simple and real for the readers.

Vijay Kasireddy, CEO of Fiind Inc., – for being a great source of strength who keeps pushing our entire team to raise the bar at Fiind. A sincere thanks to Vijay, for taking out the time for a brilliant Foreword.

Vinod Muthukrishnan, CEO of Cloudcherry, for being that friend who pulls no punches and gives you constructive feedback and relishes your success.

Acknowledgements

Anjan Cariappa, for creating amazing illustrations despite his schedule as a serial entrepreneur.

Christian Fictoor, founder of iGNiTE Music and FPI Consulting, who contributed a lot in conceptualizing this book and for writing the last word for this book.

Notion Press, for being my extended family and exhibiting great professionalism. Your suggestions have been invaluable.

And the list goes on.

Author Bio

 Yaagneshwaran Ganesh is the Director of Marketing at Fiind Inc., a Seattle-based predictive intelligence startup powered by machine learning. He is known for his critically acclaimed book *Is Your Marketing in Sync or Sinking?*

Yaagneshwaran is also a speaker on global forums, a columnist and an active member of the startup ecosystem. He has served as a consultant and sounding board to startups in the Asia Pacific and Europe.

This book is a manifestation of his quest as a marketing enthusiast urging you to not just be an influencer, but be a syncfluencer without burning cash.

You can contact him on:
Twitter: @yaagneshwaran
Email: yaagneshwaran@fiind.com

www.ingramcontent.com/pod-product-compliance
Lightning Source LLC
Chambersburg PA
CBHW020437220526
45464CB00002B/738